A CourseGuide for

Five Views on the
Apostle Paul

**Michael F. Bird,
Thomas R. Schreiner,
Luke Timothy Johnson,
Douglas A. Campbell,
Mark D. Nanos**

ZONDERVAN
ACADEMIC

ZONDERVAN ACADEMIC

A CourseGuide for Four Views on the Apostle Paul

Copyright © 2020 by Zondervan

Requests for information should be addressed to:
Zondervan, *3900 Sparks Dr. SE, Grand Rapids, Michigan 49546*

ISBN 978-0-310-11056-9 (softcover)

CONTENTS

Introduction

Welcome to *A CourseGuide for Four Views on the Apostle Paul*. These guides were created for formal and informal students alike who want to engage deeper in biblical, theological, or ministry studies. We hope this guide will provide an opportunity for you to grow not only in your understanding, but also in your faith.

How to Use This Guide

This guide is meant to be used in conjunction with the book *Four Views on the Apostle Paul* and its corresponding videos, *Four Views on the Apostle Paul, A Video Study*. After you have read each chapter in the book and watched the accompanying video lesson, the materials in this guide will help you review and assess what you have learned. Application-oriented questions are included as well.

Each CourseGuide has been individually designed to best equip you in your studies, but in general, you can expect the following components. Most CourseGuides begin every chapter with a "You Should Know" section, which highlights key terminology, people, and facts to remember. This section serves as a helpful summary for directing your studies. Reflection questions, typically two to three per chapter, prompt you to summarize key points you've learned. Discussion questions invite you to an even deeper level of engagement. Finally, most chapters will end with a short quiz to test your retention. You can find the answer key to each quiz at the bottom of the page following it.

For Further Study

CourseGuides accompany books and videos from some of the world's top biblical and theological scholars. They may be used independently, or in small groups or classrooms, offering quality instruction to equip students for academic and ministry pursuits. If you would like to engage in further study with Zondervan's CourseGuides, the full lineup may be viewed online. After completing your studies with *A CourseGuide for Four Views on the Apostle Paul*, we recommend moving on to *A CourseGuide for Five Views on Biblical Inerrancy* and *A Course-Guide for Faith Alone*.

Introduction to Four Views on the Apostle Paul

1. Explain why Paul is described as both "inspirational" and "incendiary," both in his own lifetime and today.

2. Explain the viewpoint of Thomas R. Schreiner with respect to Paul as it is described in the introduction. What are the key aspects and accents of Schreiner's views on Paul?

3. Discuss as fully as you can based on the introduction the position and views on Paul of either Luke Timothy Johnson or Douglas A. Campbell.

4. According to the introduction, what sets Mark D. Nanos apart from the other three scholars? What intrigues you about his contribution to this collaboration? What are you the most curious about learning from Nanos, and why?

CHAPTER 1

Paul: A Reformed Reading (Thomas Schreiner)

You Should Know

- Schreiner says Paul's theology was based on the Old Testament.

- Paul was convinced the Old Testament should be read as pointing to Christ and thought those who failed to see Christ as its fulfillment were blinded by sin.

- For Paul, the coming of Christ marked both the fulfillment of prophecy and the revelation of mystery.

- According to the Old Testament, the coming of the Spirit signifies the advent of the new creation.

- Paul uses "Lord" in reference to both the Father and the Son, showing that he identifies Jesus with God the Father. Paul does not carefully distinguish between the lordship of God and Christ.

- *Christus Victor*: An atonement theory that describes Christ as triumphant over the devil and demonic powers through his work on the cross

- Forensic righteousness: the righteousness accorded to believers by virtue of God's just, legal declaration by which he bestows upon them the righteousness of Christ

- *Pistis Christou*: Greek phrase meaning either "faith in Christ" (objective genitive) or "faith of Christ" (subjective genitive); Thomas R. Schreiner defends the objective genitive interpretation of this phrase, while Luke Timothy Johnson suggests both meanings are clearly found in Paul

- Replacement theology: the belief that the church has superseded the Jews as God's chosen people

Essay Questions

Short

1. According to Schreiner, is worshiping Jesus Christ in tension with monotheism in Paul's view? Why or why not, and how does Paul demonstrate this in his language concerning Jesus?

2. How does Schreiner describe Paul's understanding of God's wrath and judgment, both in the eschaton and in the present?

3. What do you think Schreiner means by a "forensic" reading of justification? How does he defend such an interpretation of justification?

Long

1. The theme of "already but not yet" pervaded Schreiner's essay on many points. Explain this idea of inaugurated eschatology with reference to Christ's life, death, and resurrection; prophecy/fulfillment and mystery/revelation; salvation; and the church. Why do you think Schreiner returns to this idea throughout his essay? What are some key implications for Christians today?

2. Which response to Schreiner's essay do you think provided the most compelling critique? Explain that scholar's critique of Schreiner. Why do you find it compelling? How do you think Schreiner would respond?

Response Essay Questions

1. Why does Luke Timothy Johnson take issue with Schreiner locating the framework for Paul's thought in Old Testament Scripture? How does Johnson believe this characterization falls short?

2. What does Douglas A. Campbell mean when he describes Schreiner's views as Melancthonian? Describe what this view means in regard to justification and atonement. Why does Campbell find this view problematic?

3. How does Mark D. Nanos respond to Schreiner's claim that, for Paul, the church of Jesus Christ constitutes the "true" Israel? What does Nanos mean by "replacement theology," and how does it factor into his critique of Schreiner?

Quiz

1. (T/F) Judaism in the Second Temple period was influenced significantly by Hellenism.

2. (T/F) According to Schreiner, Paul believes that the new age has been consummated in Christ.

3. Thomas R. Schreiner says Paul's theology was derived from:
    a) Gnosticism
    b) The Old Testament
    c) Hellenism
    d) The Enochic tradition

4. Which Old Testament prophet foretold God's "new covenant"?

    a) Isaiah
    b) Jeremiah
    c) Hosea
    d) Daniel

5. What event indicates to Paul that the new creation has dawned?

    a) Christ's birth
    b) Christ's death
    c) Christ's resurrection
    d) The outpouring of the Spirit

6. Which epistle mentions outside teachers who insisted Gentiles be circumcised to become part of God's people, according to Schreiner's interpretation?

a) Colossians
b) 1 Corinthians
c) Galatians
d) Romans

7. According to Schreiner, how would Paul answer the question of why salvation is needed?

a) To save humans from sin and the wrath of God
b) To restore humans to their original state of glory
c) To liberate humans from the oppressive powers and authorities
d) To demonstrate the victory of God over Satan and evil

8. Romans 5:12–19 traces sin and death to:

a) Adam
b) Noah
c) Satan
d) Babel

9. Which best characterizes Luke Timothy Johnson's evaluation of Thomas R. Schreiner's essay?

a) Too strongly influenced by the historical-critical method
b) Firmly Baptist, to the point of near total exclusion of Roman Catholics from God's people
c) Familiar to most Christians, but highly selective when checked against the entire Pauline correspondence
d) Too freighted by the stagnant Reformed theology of Old Princeton to meaningfully speak to the concerns of today

10. How does Douglas A. Campbell characterize Schreiner's view of salvation?

a) Melancthonian
b) Calvinist
c) Wesleyan
d) Zwinglian

CHAPTER 2

The Paul of the Letters: A Catholic Perspective (Luke Timothy Johnson)

You Should Know

- The "undisputed" letters of Paul: Romans, 1 Corinthians, 2 Corinthians, Galatians, Philippians, 1 Thessalonians, and Philemon

- The "disputed" letters of Paul: 1 Timothy, 2 Timothy, Titus, Colossians, Ephesians, and 2 Thessalonians

- Seven of the Pauline letters are regarded as authentic, or actually written by Paul himself, according to broad scholarly consensus. The other six are disputed in their authorship, to a greater or lesser degree.

- Paul speaks of Jesus as the last Adam.

- By the standards of the Torah, Jesus's death made him cursed by God.

- Types of language in which metaphors Paul uses to describe salvation are expressed: diplomatic language, economic language, forensic language, cultic language, kinship language

- *Kyrios*: Greek for "Lord"; the LXX uses this word for the proper name of God; Paul also uses the term to refer to Jesus Christ

- *Kenōsis*: Greek for "emptying out"; the way in which Christ does not regard being in the form of God as "something to be grasped" but takes on the form of humans as an expression of humility

- *Ekklēsia*: Greek for "church"; this word appears in all of Paul's letters except for 2 Timothy and Titus

Essay Questions

Short

1. What does Johnson mean when he writes about the "search for a center" in Paul's thought? What are some examples of this that he points to? Why does he say each attempt fails to meet the evidentiary test?

2. Johnson describes five metaphors Paul uses to explain salvation, drawing from the social and religious realities of Greco-Roman and Jewish culture. List and explain three of them.

3. What does Johnson mean by saying Paul is not a systematic but a practical or pastoral theologian? How is this reflected in Paul's correspondence?

Long

1. Summarize Johnson's lengthy description of the identity, role, and nature of the church. What external and internal tensions plagued the church? How does Johnson describe Paul's approach to the internal tensions, and does this differ from Campbell's response on this point?

2. Thomas R. Schreiner expressed his deep agreement with Johnson on many points. However, Mark D. Nanos had a rather more positive valuation of Johnson than of Schreiner. How do you account for this? Why do you think Johnson's essay received praise from both scholars? How do you imagine a conversation between the three of them would go, and why?

Response Essay Questions

1. Explain why Schreiner believes a strong focus on Paul's social location and history has some liabilities. What shortcomings does he believe this leads to in Johnson's essay?

2. What does Campbell find unsatisfying in what Johnson writes regarding these codes?

3. How does Nanos differ from Johnson in his analysis of Paul's thought on Jewish Christians following the commandments (Torah)? Why?

Quiz

1. (T/F) Luke Timothy Johnson thinks Acts is indispensable for reconstructing Paul's life.

2. (T/F) Paul's letters do not contain substantial portions of gospel material.

3. (T/F) Johnson argues that forensic language is the most important salvation metaphor in Paul's letters, and it governs all the other salvation metaphors Paul uses.

4. (T/F) Johnson believes Paul's language about salvation is almost entirely social rather than individual.

5. Since the late nineteenth century, how many of Paul's letters has the scholarly consensus held to be "authentic" or actually written by Paul?

   a) None
   b) Two
   c) Seven
   d) Twelve

6. Whom does Paul describe as the last of those to whom Jesus appeared after his death?

   a) Cephas
   b) Paul
   c) John
   d) More than five hundred people

7. In Galatians and Romans, what functions as the key hermeneutical lens for reinterpretation of the Torah?

   a) Jesus's parables
   b) The Sermon on the Mount

    c) The *parousia*

    d) The cross of Christ

8. In Paul's letters, *ekklēsia* refers primarily to:

    a) The universal church

    b) The local assembly

    c) The "invisible church" of saved persons

    d) The Gentile Christian community

9. Which of the following is *not* one of Paul's primary metaphors for the church?

    a) Building

    b) Body

    c) Temple

    d) Tower

10. Which epistle does Douglas A. Campbell specifically suggest was written later than Paul's time due to its position on women?

    a) 1 Corinthians

    b) Romans

    c) Galatians

    d) 1 Timothy

Christ and the Church in Paul: A "Post-New Perspective" Account (Douglas Campbell)

You Should Know

- The new perspective on Paul is first a new perspective on Judaism.

- According to Campbell, Paul's bracketing argument in Romans 5–8 is aimed at assurance.

- Campbell says that Paul connects God's election with hope.

- Paul writes that Adam is a type of Christ in Romans 5:14.

- Campbell believes freedom in Romans 6 is developed in relational situations by the incremental creation of new possibilities for actions, which must be learned and embodied. Freedom is therefore learned and taught.

- Nanos argues Campbell wrongly conflates circumcision with Torah observance.

- The most literal English rendering of Torah is "teaching."

- Covenantal nomism: the understanding that Jews did not practice the law out of legalism but in the interest of maintaining their exclusive God-given relational status

- E. P. Sanders: the author of the 1977 book *Paul and Palestinian Judaism*; associated with initiating the new perspective on Judaism

Essay Questions

Short

1. What is covenantal nomism, in your opinion? What does it have to do with interpreting Paul? How does this understanding mark a shift from earlier, traditional interpretations?

2. What does Campbell believe results when interpreters see the "secondary" realities of sin and suffering as preceding the primary reality of the Christ event? What does he mean by this, and what is at stake in this logical ordering?

3. Do you think Campbell is a universalist (i.e., that he believes *everyone* is saved), based on his essay? Why or why not? What does he write that could be construed in this direction?

Long

1. Summarize the origins and concerns of the new perspective on Paul. What historical event and two scholarly re-evaluations lie behind the movement? How does the movement influence Campbell (what does he affirm in it), and why is he adamant about the *post* in his approach of "post-new perspective" (what does he think is lacking in the new perspective)?

2. The way Schreiner and Campbell describe God's judgment with regard to the Adam-Christ parallel is markedly different. Outline both of their views. Which view do you think fits better with Pauline material? Why?

Response Essay Questions

1. How does Schreiner challenge Campbell's analysis of Paul's Adam-Christ parallel and its implications for judgment? What view does he promote in contrast to Campbell's?

2. Summarize Luke Timothy Johnson's response to Campbell's decision to focus his essay on Romans 5–8. Why does this focus succeed or fail, in Johnson's view?

3. How does Nanos disagree with Campbell on Paul's ethical expectations for non-Jews? Why?

Quiz

1. (T/F) Campbell acknowledges that his interpretations of Paul are new and hitherto untested.

2. (T/F) Campbell affirms that Paul's thinking about God's activity in Christ is trinitarian.

3. (T/F) In the Adam-Christ parallel, Christ is the original image.

4. Which of the following best describes Douglas A. Campbell's approach to Paul?
   a) New perspective
   b) Post-new perspective
   c) Lutheran
   d) Jewish

5. Which part of Paul's writings does Campbell focus his essay upon?
   a) Romans 9–11
   b) Romans 5–8
   c) The Pastoral Epistles
   d) 1 Corinthians 9–15

6. Campbell associates humans being made in the image of God with the fact that humans are:
   a) Rational
   b) Relational
   c) Religious
   d) Creative

7. What does Paul usually call the people whom we call "Christians"?
   a) Brothers
   b) Children
   c) Followers of the Way
   d) Apostles

8. In Romans 5:12–21, Paul compares Christ and:
   a) Esau
   b) Adam
   c) David
   d) Moses

9. How does Thomas R. Schreiner suggest Campbell's view could be labeled?
   a) Lutheran
   b) Marcion
   c) Post-liberal
   d) Uber-Reformed

10. Which scholar celebrates Campbell's interest in a *post*-new perspective approach to Paul?
   a) Thomas R. Schreiner
   b) Luke Timothy Johnson
   c) Mark D. Nanos
   d) None of these

CHAPTER 4

A Jewish View
(Mark Nanos)

You Should Know

- Nanos believes the contrast between faith and deeds is a false binary.

- Nanos argues that Paul should be taken seriously as a first-century Jew rather than an apostate.

- Nanos believes using law for Torah plays into a common Christian value judgment against Judaism.

- Acts emphasizes that Paul remained a Pharisee and practiced Torah.

- Words Nanos prefer as an English option when Paul speaks of "faith": Faithfulness, loyalty, or trust

- Rather than speaking of "false teachers" in Galatians, Nanos calls them influencers.

- Johnson asserts that Nanos assumes a later form of Judaism, which developed after the composition of the Mishnah in about 200 CE, to describe the Judaism of Paul's day.

- Paulinism: a traditional construction of Christian ideals supposedly championed by Paul

- Pharisaism: the movement characterized by encouraging a highly devoted lifestyle of holiness among Jews in ways that were technically only specified for priests in Torah

Essay Questions

Short

1. According to Nanos, how does Judaism view faith without good deeds? How does this compare to the New Testament?

2. Why does Nanos prefer to speak of "Torah" rather than "law"? What does he believe are the weaknesses and subsequent implications of simply rendering this word as "law"?

3. What does Nanos posit Paul's belief was regarding his fellow Jews who did not share his perspective on Christ and the new age? How did Paul believe their status differed from that of other nations who had not yet turned to Christ? Why?

Long

1. Describe as fully as you can Nanos's view of Paul's Judaism both before and after Paul encounters Jesus. In view of this, why does Nanos like or dislike the language of Paul "converting" from Judaism to Christianity? How might his interpretation impact a Christian's reading of Paul?

2. Nanos writes that he believes his understanding of Paul offers a platform for Christians to understand Jews more respectfully and for Jews to understand Christian origins more respectfully. Having read his essay and the responses of the other three scholars, do you agree with Nanos? Why or why not? Be specific.

Response Essay Questions

1. How does Schreiner evaluate Nanos's claim of Paul's own Torah observance? How does he support his evaluation?

2. Summarize Luke Timothy Johnson's description of Judaism during Paul's lifetime. How does his description constitute a critique of Nanos?

3. Summarize Campbell's response to Nanos's evaluation of the new perspective on Paul, especially in terms of its ability to answer the "Jewish questions." Does Campbell agree with Nanos? Why or why not?

Quiz

1. (T/F) Paul makes a number of positive comments about Torah and Jewish identity.

2. (T/F) Nanos states that Judaism teaches that good deeds are motivated by an effort to be saved.

3. (T/F) Nanos believes that after Paul's Damascus road experience, Paul remains a Torah-observant Jew.

4. (T/F) According to Paul, good deeds will be rewarded.

5. (T/F) According to Nanos, Paul believed that Jews who disagreed with him about Jesus were still in the covenant.

6. (T/F) Nanos believes that Paul regards all Christians as "Israelites."

7. Which of the following sums up Mark D. Nanos's critique of the new perspective on Paul?

    a) It continues to view Judaism as legalistic
    b) It continues to approach Paul as though he stands outside Judaism
    c) It is inconsistent with Paul's obvious dislike for the law
    d) It misses that Paul associates baptism with circumcision

8. To whom does "freedom from Torah" apply, according to Nanos?

    a) All Christ-followers
    b) Non-Jews who are Christ-followers
    c) Jews who are Christ-followers
    d) Non-Christ-followers

9. Nanos challenges the contention that Paul should be considered a(n):

    a) Christ-follower
    b) Jew

c) Apostle
d) Convert

10. Nanos argues that "circumcision" in Paul's writing should be understood as metonymy for:

a) Proselyte conversion
b) Torah observance
c) Legalism
d) Ethnocentrism

Conclusion

1. Why does Michael F. Bird comment that this project does not match the general trend of "views" books, namely that they tend toward a superficial resolution? How is that *not* the case for the scholarly dialogue throughout this particular project?

2. Summarize concisely the four views of salvation promoted by the four scholars. What does salvation consist of, how is it accomplished, and what is one saved from or for?

3. Which scholar do you think received the most positive valuation overall from the other three? Why? How was this scholar able to establish areas of commonality with each of the others?

4. Between which two scholars do you sense the most lingering discord? Why? Explain from both sides of their disagreement(s).

Notes

www.ingramcontent.com/pod-product-compliance
Lightning Source LLC
Chambersburg PA
CBHW011746020426
42331CB00014B/3301